Non-Fungible Token GuideBook

Everything you need to know about NFT

Reuben Ademola

Contents

Introduction

A unique token is known as non-fungible and the idea is different from assets such as cash or gold. They are thought of as one-of-a-kind trading cards. The cards can be duplicated in any way but they are not the real thing. Basically, NFT is a cryptographic token that is a unique asset on a blockchain. They are fully digital assets or partial versions of the real-world assets as tokens. Because they are not interchangeable with each other, they operate as proof of authenticity and ownership in the digital space.

To further break it down, when an asset's individual units are interchanged and are not quite different from each other, they are described as fungible. An example is fiat currency because each unit can replace or substitute another equivalent unit.

If you have a ten-dollar bill, it is interchangeable with another genuine ten-dollar bill.

It is a special principle for an asset that intends to be used as a medium of exchange.

When a currency is fungible, it is an attractive property since it allows free exchange and regardless of where you got your own ten-dollar bill or twenty-dollar bill, the amount is valid in the market and where the units came from is particularly irrelevant. For collectible items, knowing the history of each individual unit is the bedrock of the system.

What happens now if we create digital assets that is similar to Bitcoin, and then we go a step further by including a unique identifier to each unit? In essence, one unit of the same value will be different to another. That idea is what NFT is basically.

What is the uproar about tracking assets and creating non-fungible tokens? Regular tokens that were created under the ERC-20 standard are divisible and interchangeable.

The property for tracking unique assets is completely irrelevant to us because we are not looking at dividing our digital image or a car into several tokens for the purpose of distribution. This underlying principle destroys the idea behind non-fungible tokens because we want just one of them attributed to a single asset.

Duplicating and dividing tokens disapproves our intention to define them with a unique attribute or property. That is where non-fungible tokens come in to subvert the interchangeability issue. A regular ERC-20 token can be substituted for another ERC20 token. ERC-721 solves this property problem once again.

Each NFT token tracks a different asset, turns it to an immutable value that cannot be changed or substituted with another asset. Traders may easily trade digital assets that are fungible, besides ownership of an asset cannot be proved once it has changed hands a couple of times. This is the main reason why non-fungible tokens have been created.

Characteristics of Non-fungible Token

These are the properties of NFT

- Uniqueness
- Rarity
- Indivisibility

Uniqueness

Assets are defined and are assigned with metadata which further describes the asset and differentiates it from other assets. Let us take an example, a project called Decentraland that sells virtual pieces of land. The metadata assigns unique description to each piece of land that includes such information as coordinates and perhaps the percentage of land covered by grass or the type of building that it has.

Rarity

This element is also called scarcity and it is what makes NFTs so popular. Token developers under the traditional ERC20 define the limits of the token. If you want to supply 1,000,000 tokens, you simply set that boundary. Do you want more tokens? Freely increase the aggregate in your smart contract. Although, depending on the algorithm that you use, different rules may apply on its possibility and entire prohibition.

Another thing with NFTs is the impossibility to create an infinity pool of new assets. The rarity principle ensures that each asset is defined one time on the blockchain, a particular attribute of NFTs among collectors. In essence, another individual cannot register the same asset another time, therefore assets are technically hard to come by.

Rarity is a valuable bedrock of NFTs as an economic platform for people looking to purchase them. Because all assets are immutable and have unique attribution, you can own a piece of land in a game and trade it just like you would a piece of land.

Indivisibility

NFTs cannot be divided. For example, if you have a bitcoin i.e., 1 bitcoin. If you don't have enough money to purchase 1 bitcoin, you can spread it out in fractions, 1/10 of a bitcoin such as smaller denominations called satoshis or units. To expand on the bitcoin example, let us assume that you wish to stop users from buying 10% of a train ticket. If bitcoin had non-fungible characteristics, buying 1 bitcoin is only the choice that you ever had.

How do Non-Fungible Tokens work?

Ethereum released the ERC-721 standard that permits developers to define unique assets. The ERC-721 standard was completed on January 24, 2018 and it defines the functions for Ethereum contracts to become valid. Let us take a quick dive into the ERC-721 metadata contract to see the amazing functionality first hand.

If we are defining an NFT, we can attach a name and symbol. Furthermore, we can also create a URL that embeds a JSON file which further describes the unique properties of the NFT. A JSON file is one form of data notation that records properties such as name, description, and an attached image to expand on the description and the unique identity of the NFT.

There are several frameworks to create and release NFTs.

The most popular among them is a standard for the issuance and trading of non-fungible assets directly on the Ethereum blockchain. Apart from the ERC-721 issuance standard, there is a better one called the ERC-1155.

It allows a single contract to have both fungible and no-fungible tokens, that further expands the possibilities for developers and the whole industry. To fully cement the standardization of NFTs, there is a higher degree of interoperability that adds value to the users at the backend. This concept means that unique assets are exchanged between different applications easily.

If you are storing and want to see your NFTs, just maneuver to the Trust Wallet. You will find your NFT on an address like other blockchain tokens. Remember that NFTs are immutable and cannot also be transferred without the consent of the owner.

If you are interested in trading NFTs, hit the open marketplaces such as OpenSea.

This is the place where buyers are connected with sellers, and of course the value of each token is unique. NFTs are prone to changes in price because of the changes in market supply and demand. Where does it get its value? The object just like money does not have any inherent value, only what people assign its value to be.

Basically, value is a shared belief. That it is fiat money, precious metals, or vehicles, these things don't matter until people add value to them. This is the short explanation of how an item becomes valuable, why not digital collectibles?

What are NFTs used for?

Decentralized applications (DApps) use it to issue digital items and crypto-collectibles. The tokens are a collectible item, an investment product, or any other valuable material. They have found a good landing spot in the gaming industry that is expanding by the day.

Because several of the games played online have individual economies, tokenizing gaming assets with blockchain is a breath of fresh air to take things further. Using NFTs could solve or reduce the problem of inflation suffered by several online games.

Also, NFTs can be used to tokenize real-world assets which are an expansion on its application into the virtual world.

NFTs could represent fractions of real-world assets stored and traded as tokens on a blockchain and serve as immediate liquidity to several cash-strapped markets such as fine art, real estate, rare collectible items and several others.

The intuitive properties of NFTs will also add value to the digital identity sector where storing identification and data ownership on the blockchain would enhance security and privacy. Besides data of several people all over the world will be guaranteed.

Because it is very easy to move assets from one part of the globe to another, there will be less friction in the global economy.

NFTs and DeFi

The potential of NFTs will be greatly felt in the evolving world of decentralized finance where fine art, real estate, or other valuable assets can be used as collateral for loans or financial contracts for insurance, stock options or bonds that are exchanged as products on secondary markets.

NFTs are also used as governance tokens for NFT marketplaces. It is likely that the growth of decentralized finance will make NFTs more attractive as a digital assets options that has a range of applications.

Why NFTs are important

The buzz around NFTs is usually downplayed, but it should not. NFTs are used to obtain and exchange ownership of physical assets in a digital marketplace because they are a fool-proof record of digital real-world asset.

There is potential there to disrupt the rare and valuable items market and industry.

Once an NFT is minted on the blockchain and its unique content attached, the owner has proven to be the sole holder of the token, which means that the asset not only is unique but also scarce.

If NFTs are applied to the music industry, there is a disruptive potential there for indie artists that have struggled so far to successfully monetize their streaming content and even the music industry as a whole. RAIR, a digital rights management platform thinks that NFTs can be used to license and distribute the content of musicians.

Adding smart contracts to that, artists will continue to earn royalties when their work is resold another time. Remember that the transfer of NFT ownership does not transfer a trademark or copyright to the holder.

The creator also uploads several versions of a work piece, each identified and attributed with unique NFTs. In essence, it is not a one-off distribution thing.

In the gaming industry, NFTs hold a huge promise where the reality of in-game economies is a near possibility. Game players can claim rare or difficult items using their NFTs as part of rewards for completing challenges and participating in special events. The possibilities are endless. Game developers can also use NFTs to monetize their product from players.

NFTs hold an attractive value for investors because they can be bought and sold for a profit. Even traditional asset organizations and investment firms are laying their claim to NFTs and purchasing digital collectibles to create value for their clients. There is more to NFTs and a potential for innovation in digital economy.

Since cryptocurrency prices catapulted to new heights crushing earlier ceilings, the popularity of NFTs also exploded in late 2020.

An analysis done by NonFungible.com identifies the total volume of NFTs traded in 2020, with in-game transactions and sales, increased by 299%. Basically, there was an increase from $62.9m to $250.8m in 2019. Also, the number of active wallets increased from 112,731 to 222,179 just the previous year.

There is a positive indication that sales will accelerate and improve as more artists and brands pour in to use NFTs against the traditional routes of financial institution to market and monetize their products directly to buyers.

How are NFTs created?

"Minting" is how NFTs are created which is a metaphor to the process of creating a physical coin. NFTs are minted on an NFT marketplace, where a creator uploads a digital file and attributes unique features, such as duplication, and a part or a collection among others.

When the NFT is created, the owner may choose to sell it on the marketplace through an exchange or basically auction it off. NFTs run on the Ethereum blockchain, but the WAX blockchain can mint digital tokens that creators have in one way or the other attributed files. How to purchase NFTs?

Why we need non-fungible tokens?

One major reason is that NFTs work as seamless financial solutions for several digital economies. In the gaming industry, that boasts of active hub of micro-economies, games such as CS:GO, League of Legends, or Fortnite: Battle Royale. These games run a small economy of in-game assets that are traded amongst players. Even players receive in-game assets for completing a challenge such as new skins for their avatar and stickers for their weapon.

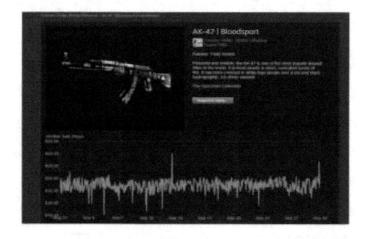

In the figure above, gamers show interest in paying money to receive a beautiful skin that improves their gameplay immersion and experience.

Although, in reality, the gamers do not have full proprietary rights on the assets, the game developer continues to control the price for in-game assets or modify a specific to cause a drop in demand and consequently price. An experience that is common with CSGO skins in the past.

The possibility that gamers can deploy a feature or resource such as a weapon or avatar skin across different genre of games will become a reality soon which further expands the potential of inter-game economies.

Because identity movement is becoming decentralized, a benefit of NFT is that physical properties like a house can then be linked to your decentralized identity where it becomes a valid proof of ownership to exchange assets in a global market.

Which Projects Heavily Rely On Nfts?

Several projects have adopted and introduced NFTs. Some of them are prominent and popular adopters of this technology.

Cryptokitties

The very first adoption of NFTs in the mainstream media was demonstrated by Cryptokitties. It shares almost the same concept with Pokemon Go. You collect digital crypto cats that come with striking differences just like you collect Pokemons with unique characteristics. By breeding cats, you expand the differences and create new cats and new differences.

Decentraland

It is a virtual world where you can own a piece of virtual land. You get to further develop your piece of land and plant cool structures on it. These new information and development go in to your NFT's metadata. The game let you trade virtual land with other gamers to create larger communities to share in the virtual experience.

Gods Unchained

If you had played card games like Yu-Gi-Oh and exchanged with your friends a few times, you will remember that you attempted to complete your collection. Just like other collectors like you that listed their cards on eBay and other marketplaces online in a bid to complete their special card collection. It is relatively easy now but back in the days, it was quite difficult to trade and collect cards. Card collectors were encumbered with uncertainties such as

- What happens if I pay for a card and don't receive it?
- How can I get a chargeback if the card I bought online is fake?
- How to prove the ownership of a card after purchasing it?

One huge card collection project that put gamers at ease has been created by Gods Unchained. The cards are issued as NFTs. Ownership of the cards can therefore be digitally transferred, thereby solving the concerns above. Besides, the authenticity of each card can be verified. You can also exchange ownership of cards through an easy Ethereum transaction.

NBA TOP SHOTS

The most popular platform for NFTs is none other than NBA Top Shots that was built on the FLOW blockchain. It captured historic moments from several NBA competitions where the reaction is then minted into NFTs.

Tokens have varying rarity, not to the same degree. For example, you will see a few minted NFTs that captured moments that are available in small volumes while others appear in thousands. As investors begin to hit the market, a lot of the minted NFTs are increasing in value daily.

Because of the hype, the platform has benefited immensely from the buzz surrounding their packs, sometimes up to a thousand people subscribe to a waiting list to get into the frenzy.

OpenSea Marketplace for NFTs

Last but not the least is the OpenSea marketplace, that encourages NFTs to be auctioned. OpenSea is basically a decentralized marketplace that supports trading with a smart contract. You can trade more than 200 types of NFTs, such as CryptoKitties, SuperRare art, Gods Unchained cards, and domain names for Ethereum.

My Crypto Heroes

It is a multiplayer role-playing game (RPG) where players level up their historical characters by participating in quests and battles. On the Ethereum blockchain, the heroes and items in the game are delivered as tokens.

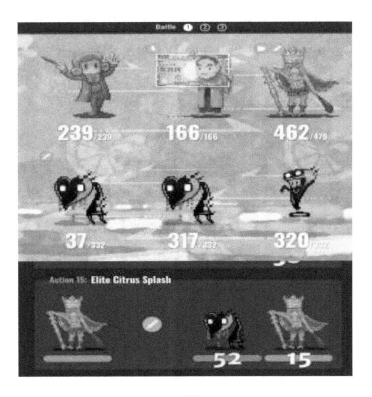

Binance Collectibles

These are NFTs that are issued in support of Binance and Enjin, although the collaboration of both cypto financial markets is infrequent. Follow Binance on Twitter to get one of those and anticipate subsequent giveaways. If you want to be part of the NFT giveaway, do the following:

- Download an Ethereum wallet or one that supports it, such as Trust Wallet.
- Copy your Ethereum address and follow the giveaway rules. Submit as a form or simply as a comment on Twitter, go over the rules to understand the requirements for the giveaway.
- When you win an NFT and it is distributed, check it below the Collectibles tab in Trust Wallet. Thereafter, you may choose to either HODL, or sell those at a P2P marketplace like OpenSea.

-

Binance collectibles on Enjin

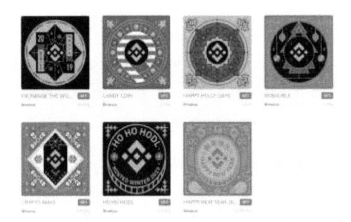

Crypto Stamps

The Austrian Postal Service issue the Crypto Stamps and act as a bridge that connects the virtual world to reality. The stamps are used to move or exchange mail just like any other stamp. The difference is that they are recorded as digital images on the Ethereum blockchain, which identifies them as a digital asset to be traded as a digital collectible.

How to Buy NFTs?

Before you learn how to buy NFTs, let us talk about a few popular marketplaces that are killing it with NFTs. We mentioned OpenSea earlier, the other one is Rarible.

To buy an NFT on OPenSea, connect a compatible wallet running on the ERC-721 standard, one is MetaMask.

Their user interface is seen in the image above. Towards the left, there are trending collections. So you will have to check or filter to find what you are looking for. Under each NFT, the validity of the auction period before elapsing is displayed. In the example below, we selected the first NFT, the Wrapped Mooncat.

The buying page of a selected NFT looks like the one above. The information or the properties of the NFT are displayed there such as price history, the creator, a little description of the NFT, and current offers below. There are two things that you can do here:

The first one is to purchase the NFT directly for the price that was listed for it. In the image and the example above, it is 0,9999

ETH. To participate in the auction, tap "make an offer" with the button under it. Once your offer is accepted, your Ethereum account is immediately debited and you are credited with the NFT.

What are the obvious risks?

NFTs are not raising any eyebrows or ruffling feathers at the moment because they are just gaining momentum. The value of Tokens is hooked on what people perceive them to be. They are like autographs. At the moment, there is a huge bubble as a result of the buzz around it and of course the likely danger to the environment.

The latter has caused several critics to attempt to crash the cryptocurrency bandwagon because of its ridiculous carbon footprint that is not ending soon. Bitcoin network consumes power that can serve the country of Chile annually.

It also produces electronic waste to the degree produced by Luxembourg. The same can be said of NFTs as they run on blockchain technology. A single Ethereum transaction consumes about 61kWh, to put it into perspective, that is the energy an average American household consumes in two days.

NFTs and Beyond

You may want to ask why NFTs had so much value? It is the same incredulous reaction when a painting is valued at 1,000 euros. Imagine paying $1,000 for an abstract painting erroneously from an artist who claimed that it was original and from way back.

A painting that you cannot prove its authenticity, what if it is a counterfeit? Imagine owning a digital painting that attributes you as the sole owner and you are able to prove its authenticity too.

The idea is that value or perceived value is relative, and the value of NFT rests on how much one is willing to pay for it just like any collectible item. The value is not inherent, it is rather attributed by those that think it is valuable. Value is a shared belief after all.

A few NFTs have quad-tripled in value. One is Beeple's "The First 5,000 Days" NFT that sold for $69 million.

Conclusion

NFTs popularity over the years was the result of the authentication of both physical and digital items and the ability to proof ownership. Also, NFTs let user transfer ownership which eliminates fraud. If you purchase an NFT, the underlying asset does not belong to you. It may not bother digital assists, as NFTs are another avenue of passive income.

Investors on the other hand should be cautious. With the intervention of brick-and-mortar big guns such as Nike and Louis Vuitton, that are looking at jumping on the bandwagon, their participation is a social proof and a reprieve that will inspire legitimacy and participation in digital assets. By far the good news is that digital collectibles demonstrate the power of blockchain technology beyond conventional financial capacity.

Not only are NFTs representing physical assets in the digital space, they also demonstrate their importance as part of the blockchain ecosystem and the global economy.

Their applications are limitless and developers will create new, exciting apps and innovations in the nearest future.